USING CRAFTS IN MINISTRY

Linda and Jackie Hutto

Woman's Missionary Union®
Birmingham, Alabama

Woman's Missionary Union
P. O. Box 830010
Birmingham, AL 35283-0010

Printed in the United States of America

For more information, visit our Web site at www.wmu.com or call 1-800-968-7301.

Dewey Decimal Classification: 745.5
Subject Headings: ARTS AND CRAFTS
DECORATIVE ARTS
HANDICRAFT
MISSION ACTION

Design by Linda Hutto and Janell E. Young
Cover design by Cheryl Totty and Janell E. Young

ISBN: 1-56309-343-X
W004102•0900•5M1

Contents

Introduction

You're someone special!
We're thinking of you.
Get well soon.
Welcome to our neighborhood!
I'm glad we're friends.
You're not alone.

If you are involved in Christian missions and ministry, these are some of the expressions you hope to convey through your actions and your words. Now you can create sentimental treasures to use in your ministry efforts that also convey these feelings.

Bookstores are full of good craft books with countless ideas you can adapt in missions and ministry settings. So, how is this book different? In some ways, it is just like other crafts books you can find: it contains ideas, supply lists, instructions, photographs, and patterns. But this book also offers practical suggestions for intentionally incorporating crafts into ministry activities of all kinds involving people of all ages. Simply making a craft to give to someone can enhance your personal ministry with and witness to that person. You can make quality crafts to sell and use the proceeds to help fund missions trips and projects. Teaching others how to do a particular craft can in itself be a ministry and can lead to relationships that offer opportunities to express the gospel message. And crafts are often an important part of short-term missions trips.

This book provides craft ideas that anyone can do, using low-cost and readily available supplies, many of which you can find around your home, in thrift stores, at garage sales, and at dollar stores. Using the easy-to-follow, step-by-step instructions, you can make crafts that say, "I care."

Crafts as a personal ministry

Who can benefit from a personally made craft, or who might enjoy learning to make a craft? Consider, but don't limit yourself to, individuals in the following groups and places:

- Residents of nursing homes and assisted living facilities
- Caregivers for terminally or chronically ill patients
- Residents of halfway houses
- Residents of shelters for women and children
- Clients and volunteers in soup kitchens
- Foster families
- Those who have been temporarily relocated: military families; international students and business people; migrant workers
- Hospital patients and their families
- Patients in rehabilitation facilities
- Those experiencing a crisis pregnancy
- New neighbors and friends

- Children and teachers in preschool and day-care facilities
- Elementary school students and teachers
- Residents of low-cost housing developments and apartment complexes
- Inmates at prisons and correctional facilities (Many might enjoy learning to make a craft they can, in turn, make with their children when they visit.)

Still need a few ideas?

Consider these:

- One family had an elderly grandparent who never learned to read or write, but she loved to send and receive mail. Someone prepared a gift basket for her and included handmade cards and envelopes, along with stamps. They offered to help her write notes and letters.
- One group made Easter baskets for young men in a drug rehabilitation program. A worker in the program expressed extreme gratitude for the gesture, remarking that no one had ever done anything for these young men before.
- A church-sponsored a contest for families and other small groups to make original gingerbread houses. Once they finished the houses, they displayed them, auctioned them off, and used the money for a ministry project.
- Many neighborhood and church groups make "new neighbor" baskets that include maps, coupons, activity lists, important phone numbers, and a craft item.
- Patients undergoing long-term treatment for cancer have a variety of needs. While nutrition is especially important, treatments often make the patient's mouth sore; as a result, they do not want to eat. Gift baskets including cans of nutritional supplements, inspirational books and magazines, and a personal note offering to provide a complete meal when they feel better will brighten a cancer patient's day.
- Many times, cancer patients undergoing treatment lose their hair. Some individuals and groups regularly purchase soft, washable terry cloth skullcaps and embellish them with silk flowers, ribbons, and other decorative elements.
- Soft, handmade pillows (4-by-6-inch) offer comfort and aid for mastectomy patients, who can place these under their arms.
- Make a variety of craft items and take them to a nursing home or other residential facility where residents have limited incomes. Offer the items for the residents to "purchase" free as Christmas gifts for their family members and friends. Provide wrapping paper, tape, and name tags, and assist them with wrapping.

- Search the Web for ministry ideas. Sites such as www.getinvolved.net and www.volunteermatch.org allow individuals to enter their ZIP Codes to find opportunities in their area.

- Caps for Kids (for more information, call the Craft Yarn Council at 1-800-662-9999) is a national, nonprofit foundation that collects handmade caps for underprivileged children. Yarn shops across the country collect the caps, which are then distributed in the communities of registered stores.

Crafts as part of a missions trip or project

Many missions volunteers regularly use crafts as they teach and lead others to understand more about God's love. Including crafts as part of your missions experience can be rewarding and fun. Keep in mind the following, particularly as you travel to other locations for your missions experiences.

- Be prepared. Take all of the necessary steps in planning and preparation, even if you are an experienced crafter and an experienced missions volunteer.

- Choose projects that are relatively simple. Find out as much as you can about the people who will be working on your craft project. In the context of a larger missions assignment, some people may lack the focus to complete their tasks because of the excitement and challenge of new places, new experiences, and some times surprising emotional and spiritual growth. Plan craft projects that you can reasonably expect your coworkers to help you complete.

- Allow enough time to complete the project. Schedules are always tight in missions settings, particularly if your time frame is short (a week, or a weekend, for example). Be aware of the schedule of the entire missions project and where the crafts project fits into the larger picture. Budget your time accordingly.

- Set reasonable expectations. While you want your crafts to be the best you can produce, avoid expecting others always to meet your standards in areas such as neatness, perfection, success, quantity, and quality.

- Expect the unexpected. In spite of your best efforts and finely tuned plans, you will encounter difficulties and unexpected situations. Assignments can change at the last minute and sometimes without any warning. Sometimes situations and accommodations change when you arrive on the missions field; often needs change when you meet those with whom you will work.

- Flexibility is essential in mission settings, and your crafts projects may have to take a backseat in your overall greater purpose. If plans change unexpectedly, keep all of your supplies and plans ready for the next opportunity and stay focused on the work you need to do. You may also consider leaving your supplies and instructions for the group to use at a later time.

Assembling basic craft supplies

Note that each craft idea in this book includes a complete list of items you need to make it. If you or a group in your church plan to engage in ministry using crafts on a long-term basis, you may want to consider compiling the following supplies and storing them in a central location:

- Pencils, pens, crayons, markers
- Glues: white school glue; craft glue; roll-on adhesive (temporary and permanent); spray adhesive
- Tapes: clear adhesive; masking; plastic (colored, electrical)
- Paper: white; construction; butcher paper; colored craft paper; brown paper
- Scissors (various sizes and types, including specialty scissors)
- Pins, needles, and thread
- Hole punches (single, 3-hole, specialty)
- Hot glue guns and sticks
- Assorted foam brushes
- Assorted art brushes
- Assorted paints
- Stamps and ink pads
- Glitter
- Sandpaper
- Craft knives and blades
- Tools such as snips, wire cutters, awls, and hammers
- Rulers, templates, etc.
- Stickers
- Fabric scraps
- Ribbons, laces, etc.
- Felt (squares and by the yard)
- Elastic (various sizes)
- Velcro (adhesive-back and sew-on; varying widths and colors)
- Buttons
- Yarns
- Stuffing (old pantyhose, plastic foam packing material, beans, rice, foam sheeting, fiberfill)
- Beads
- String, twine, lacing, etc.
- Leather
- Chenille stems (pipe cleaners)
- Craft sticks (wide and narrow)
- Cardboard (various weights and sizes)
- Wood scraps
- Nature items (pine cones, dried flowers, rocks, shells, etc.)
- Modeling clay

- Wallpaper samples or leftovers
- Adhesive papers (clear and decorative)
- Disposable foam and plastic plates
- Empty spools
- Empty paper towel and bathroom tissue rolls
- Empty jars and cans
- Coffee cans with lids
- Egg cartons
- First-aid kit
- Storage boxes
- Flat boxes or portfolios
- Rags
- Newspaper
- Drop cloths

Additional crafting tips

• Store and label your craft supplies carefully.

• Before you begin work on a project, cover your work surface with newspaper, butcher paper, a drop cloth, or inexpensive plastic table covering. This will make cleanup much easier.

• Work in an area that offers adequate space, lighting, and ventilation.• Take all necessary precautions. Use gloves, aprons, and masks as needed. Tie back long hair. Wear clothing that is comfortable but not loose or flowing. Remove jewelry, ties, and scarves before working.

• Keep tools clean, sharpened, and in good shape. Obtain adequate replacements for supplies and tools.

• Use duct tape to cover cords while tools are in use to prevent someone from tripping.

• Clean up as you go.

• Most importantly, keep a proper motivation: "Whatever you say or do should be done in the name of the Lord Jesus, as you give thanks to God the Father because of him" (Col. 3:17 CEV).

bath salts

What you need:

- ½ cup baking soda
- ½ cup sea salt
- mixing bowl
- wooden spoon
- decorative jar with lid
- decorative paper and pen for tag

What you do:

1. Pour all ingredients in mixing bowl and mix well with wooden spoon.
2. Pour mixture into clean, dry jar. Seal tightly.
3. Decorate jar and add instruction tag. *Add ½ cup of the bath salts to running bath water or use the salts as a shower scrub.*

vinegar soother

What you need:

- 1 cup apple cider vinegar
- 1 cup distilled water
- stainless steel or glass pan (*not* an aluminum pan)
- funnel
- decorative bottle with lid
- decorative paper and pen for tag

What you do:

1. Pour vinegar and water into pan and cook mixture until boiling.
2. Remove pan from heat and cool completely.
3. Using a funnel, pour mixture into a clean, dry bottle. Seal tightly.
4. Decorate bottle and add instruction tag. *Apply the vinegar solution to skin with a cotton ball. The solution can also be used as a hair rinse. Pour directly onto hair and rinse thoroughly.*

"But each has a particular gift from God, one having one kind and another a different kind" (1 Cor. 7:7).

bath crystals

What you need:
- box of rock salt (used for making ice cream)
- food coloring
- 2 tablespoons glycerin or ¼ cup vegetable oil
- large mixing bowl or pan
- wooden spoon
- decorative jar with lid
- decorative paper and pen for tag

What you do:
1. Pour the rock salt in the mixing bowl.
2. Add a few drops of food coloring and stir until rock salt is well coated. Continue to add food coloring, mixing well, until salt is evenly colored. (The color will intensify when the glycerin or oil is added.)
3. Add 2 tablespoons of glycerin or ¼ cup of vegetable oil to the salt mixture. Mix well.
4. Pour the salt into a clean, dry jar and seal tightly.
5. Decorate jar and add instruction tag. *Use 1 cup of crystals in a bath of warm water.*

oatmeal scrub

What you need:
- 1 cup old-fashioned oats
- ½ cup powdered milk
- 1 tablespoon baking soda
- blender or food processor
- measuring cup and spoons
- mixing bowl
- wooden spoon
- decorative jar with lid
- decorative paper and pen for tag

What you do:
1. Blend oatmeal in a blender or food processor until it is finely ground.
2. Pour oatmeal into mixing bowl.
3. Add powdered milk and baking soda. Mix well with wooden spoon.
4. Pour mixture into clean, dry jar. Seal tightly.
5. Decorate jar and add an instruction tag.
   Small jar: *Form a paste by mixing 1 tablespoon of the oatmeal mixture with 1 tablespoon water.*
   Large bottle: *Add ½ cup of the oatmeal mixture to running bath water.*

"For we are what he has made us, created in Christ Jesus for good works, which God prepared beforehand to be our way of life" (Eph. 2:10).

foaming bath oil

What you need:
- 1 cup light vegetable oil
- ½ cup glycerin
- ½ cup mild liquid soap
- 1 tablespoon vanilla or coconut extract
- mixing bowl
- wooden spoon
- funnel
- decorative bottle with lid (8 ounces or larger)
- decorative paper and pen for tag

What you do:
1. Pour all ingredients into mixing bowl.
2. Stir with wooden spoon until well blended.
3. Using a funnel, pour mixture into a clean, dry jar or bottle. Seal tightly.
4. Decorate jar and add instruction tag. *Shake the bath oil well. Pour ¼ cup under running bath water or pour bath oil on a sponge.*

Seal decorative bottles with paraffin.

What you need:
- block paraffin
- clean coffee can
- knife
- pan
- water
- stovetop

What you do:
1. Cut paraffin into small pieces and place them in the coffee can.
2. Place the coffee can in a pan filled with 2 inches of water. This creates a double-boiler effect. **Caution: Do not place paraffin directly over heat. It is flammable!**
3. Bring water to a full boil and continue boiling until paraffin melts. Add water to the pan as needed.
4. When the paraffin has melted completely, remove pan from the heat.
5. Turn the sealed bottle upside down and dip into the melted paraffin. Dip far enough to cover the lid and rim of the bottle.
6. Let cool for 2 minutes and dip again.

"Every generous act of giving, with every perfect gift, is from above, coming down from the Father of lights, with whom there is no variation or shadow due to change" (James 1:17).

shell candles

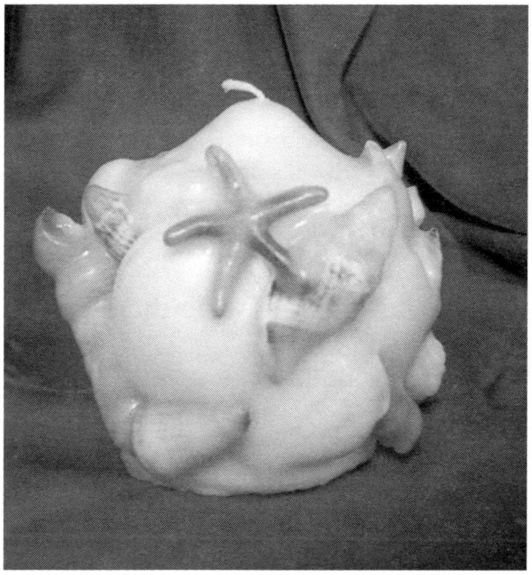

What you need:
- 3-inch pillar candle
- shells
- 2 blocks paraffin
- coffee can with lid
- hot glue gun and glue sticks
- pan
- stovetop
- pliers
- water
- waxed paper

What you do:
1. Using the glue gun, glue the shells to the candle. Press each shell in place and hold it for about 30 seconds until it is set. This is not a permanent hold, but works for this project.
2. Cut paraffin into small pieces and place them in the coffee can.
3. Add about 2 inches of water to the pan and set the coffee can in the pan of water, creating a double-boiler effect. **Caution: Do not place paraffin directly over heat. It is flammable!**
4. Heat the pan of water until it boils. Continue heating until the paraffin has melted completely.
5. Remove the pan from heat and let the paraffin cool for a few minutes.
6. Clamp the wick securely with the pliers and carefully lower the candle into melted paraffin. Cover the candle completely, but not the wick.
7. Immediately remove the candle from the paraffin and let it cool on the waxed paper for a few minutes.
8. Dip candle again and let cool completely.

"Because we look not at what can be seen but at what cannot be seen; for what can be seen is temporary, but what cannot be seen is eternal" (2 Cor. 4:18).

star candleholder

What you need:

- cat food or tuna can
- gold spray paint
- poster board
- scissors
- hot glue gun and glue sticks
- white glue
- ½-inch foam brush
- gold glitter

What you do:

1. Remove label from the can. Wash and dry it thoroughly.
2. Draw stars onto the poster board and cut them out with scissors.
3. Spray paint the can, inside and out, following the manufacturers' instructions. Allow paint to dry completely.
4. Spray paint both sides of the stars, letting each side dry thoroughly.
5. Using a foam brush, spread white glue on one side of the stars.
6. Sprinkle gold glitter over the glue.
7. Let the glue dry completely.
8. Glue the stars to the can by using the hot glue gun. Be sure that the stars do not extend below bottom of the can, preventing the can from sitting level.

Variation:

- Create seasonal candleholders using fall leaves and acorns, stars and flags for the Fourth of July, and snowflakes for winter.

"He is your praise; he is your God, who has done for you these great and awesome things that your own eyes have seen" (Deut. 10:21).

ribbon candleholder

What you need:

- cat food or tuna can
- gold spray paint
- 1⅜-inch-wide ribbon (30-inch length)
- gold cord (2 yards)
- silk leaves
- pearl beads on a stem
- white glue
- ½-inch foam brush

What you do:

1. Remove label from the can. Wash and dry it thoroughly.
2. Spray paint the can, inside and out, following the manufacturers' instructions.
3. Allow the paint to dry completely.
4. Using the foam brush, apply glue around the outside of the can.
5. Wrap ribbon around the can, pressing it securely in place.
6. Wrap gold cord around the can twice and tie it into a bow. The ribbon seam should be on the back and the bow on the front.
7. Glue the knot of the bow to the ribbon.
8. Glue silk leaves and pearl beads around the bow.

Variation:

- Glue decorative paper strips or fabric around cans. Embellish with silk flowers, twigs, nuts, or shells.

"But the Lord will be your everlasting light, and your God will be your glory" (Isa. 60:19).

candle in a cup

What you need:

- coffee or teacup
- paraffin
- white birthday candle
- white crystal glitter
- coffee can with lid
- pan
- stovetop
- oven mitt
- paper towels
- pencil
- tape

What you do:

1. Cut paraffin in small pieces and place them in the coffee can.
2. Add 2 inches of water to the pan and set the coffee can in the pan of water, creating a double-boiler effect. **Caution: Do not place paraffin directly over heat. It is flammable!**
3. Heat the pan until the water boils. Continue until the paraffin has melted completely.
4. Rinse out the cup with hot water and dry it.
5. Remove the pan from the heat.
6. Carefully pour the melted paraffin into the cup, filling the cup to within ½ inch from the top. The paraffin will settle as it cools.
7. Let the paraffin cool for a few minutes until it is slightly firm.
8. Place the birthday candle in the middle of the paraffin and hold it in place until the paraffin cools enough to set the candle.
9. Sprinkle some frosted glitter on top of paraffin.
10. Let the paraffin cool completely

Variation:

- Use a teacup and saucer. Glue the saucer to the cup and a teaspoon to the saucer. Tie a ribbon bow on the handle.

"Make your light shine, so that others will see the good that you do and will praise your Father in heaven" (Matt. 5:16 CEV).

painted candles

What you need:

- taper or stick candles
- acrylic paint (metallic colors)
- small sea sponge
- disposable foam plate
- empty egg carton
- paper
- water

What you do:

1. Turn the egg carton upside down and cut small holes in the bottom of each cup. (You will use the egg carton as a stand to hold the candles while they dry.)
2. Pour a small amount of paint onto the foam plate.
3. Wet the sea sponge and wring out as much water as possible. The sponge should be damp, not wet.
4. Dab the sponge in paint. Remove excess paint from the sponge by dabbing it on paper.
5. Holding the candle upright, paint all over the candle.
6. Place the candle in the egg carton, base down, and let it dry completely.

"'In everything do to others as you would have them do to you; for this is the law and the prophets'" (Matt. 7:12).

pearl votive candleholder

What you need:
- 9-foot pearl garland
- glass votive cup
- tacky glue
- ½-inch foam brush
- scissors

What you do:
1. Clean and dry the votive cup.
2. Using the foam brush, cover the outside of the votive cup with tacky glue.
3. Attach pearls by winding them around the cup, starting at the bottom. Be sure the rows of pearls are tight and touching.
4. After the votive cup is covered, cut off excess pearls.
5. Allow the glue to dry completely.

Variation:

Recycle votive cups from candle-type air fresheners. Embellish with strands of multicolored beads.

"'And I tell you, everyone who acknowledges me before others, the Son of Man also will acknowledge before the angels of God'" (Luke 12:8).

floral candles

What you need:

- 3-inch pillar candle
- 2- or 3-ply floral-printed napkins
- 2 blocks paraffin
- coffee can with lid
- white glue
- ½-inch foam brush
- disposable foam plate
- pan
- stovetop
- pliers
- water
- waxed paper

What you do:

1. Separate the layers of the napkin. Use only the outside printed layer for this project.
2. Tear small floral sections from the napkin.
3. Apply white glue to about ¼ of the candle with foam brush.
4. Press napkin pieces onto the candle and smooth any air bubbles.
5. Work in small areas, gluing and pressing napkin pieces onto the candle. Overlap pieces for an interesting effect.
6. Let candle dry for several hours.
7. Cut paraffin in small pieces and place them in the coffee can.
8. Add 2 inches of water to the pan and set the coffee can in the pan of water, creating a double-boiler effect. **Caution: Do not place paraffin directly over heat. It is flammable!**
9. Heat water until boiling. Continue until paraffin has melted completely.
10. Remove pan from heat and let paraffin cool for a few minutes.
11. Clamp the wick securely with pliers and carefully lower the candle into the paraffin. Cover the candle completely, but not the wick.
12. Immediately remove the candle from the paraffin and let it cool on waxed paper for 2 to 3 minutes.
13. Dip the candle again and let cool completely.

Variation:

- Glue dried flower petals or tissue paper to candles.

"'Therefore I tell you, do not worry about your life, what you will eat, or about your body, what you will wear'" (Luke 12:22).

Scripture verse prints

What you need:
- 8-by-10 frame with glass
- 8-by-10 mat (optional)
- Scripture verse (p. 62 or 63)
- parchment or other decorative paper
- 8-by-10 piece of cardboard
- clear tape
- scissors

What you do:
1. Remove the glass from the frame and clean it.
2. Photocopy the Scripture verse (p. 62 or 63) onto parchment paper.
3. Cut around the border of the verse.
4. Tape the Scripture verse to the cardboard to hold it in place.
5. Place the mat over the print.
6. Assemble the picture and attach the back of the frame.

Variation:
- Create prints with other Scripture verses, using a decorative computer font.

"A gift opens doors; it gives access to the great" (Prov. 18:16).

"families are like quilts" print

What you need:

- "Families Are Like Quilts" quote (p. 64)
- 8-by-10 frame with glass
- 8-by-10 mat
- 3-by-3 piece of quilted fabric
- parchment paper
- scissors or pinking shears
- white glue
- 8-by-10 piece of cardboard
- clear tape

What you do:

1. Remove the glass from the frame and clean it.
2. Photocopy the quote onto parchment paper.
3. Tape the parchment paper to the cardboard to hold it in place.
4. Place the mat over the paper and glue the corners of the mat to the paper.
5. Cut a heart from the 3-inch quilted fabric.
6. Position the heart on the print and glue in place.
7. Assemble the picture and attach the back of the frame.

"Devote yourselves to prayer, keeping alert in it with thanksgiving" (Col. 4:2).

decoupage frame

What you need:

- 4-by-6 or 5-by-7 frame
- magazine pages with desired colors
- white glue
- ½-inch foam brush
- 1 sheet sandpaper (220 grit)
- plastic margarine bowl and lid
- damp cloth

What you do:

1. Remove glass and backing from the frame.
2. Lightly sand the frame to dull the finish so glue will adhere.
3. Use the damp cloth to remove the dust from the frame.
4. Tear magazine pages into small pieces, the size of postage stamps.
5. Pour a small amount of glue into the margarine bowl. With the foam brush, apply glue to a small section of the frame.
6. Glue magazine pieces to the frame, pressing them flat. Work in small areas and overlap the pieces covering the entire frame and edges. Keep damp cloth handy to remove glue from fingers.
7. When frame is completely covered, smooth rough spots with your fingers and a little glue if necessary.
8. Wash brush and margarine bowl with water.
9. Let frame dry completely.
10. In the margarine bowl, mix equal parts glue and water to create a sealer. Start with ¼ cup each.
11. Brush sealer on the frame and let dry. Between coats wash the brush and place the lid on the margarine bowl.
12. Lightly sand the frame, brush on another coat of sealer, and allow the frame to dry completely.
13. Continue with as many coats of sealer as desired, lightly sanding between each coat. Do not sand final coat.
14. Clean glass and assemble frame.

Variation:

- Cover the frame with miniature candy wrappers, tissue or handmade paper, seed packets, etc.

"'I will never leave you or forsake you'" (Heb. 13:5).

creative acrylic frames

What you need:

- 5-by-7 clear acrylic frame
- corrugated paper
- tacky glue
- craft knife
- metal ruler
- pencil

What you do:

1. Lay the frame facedown on the corrugated paper. The corrugated side should be touching the frame.
2. Align the ridges of the paper with the edge of the frame to ensure a straight cut.
3. Lightly trace around the outline of the frame.
4. Use the metal ruler as a straight-edge and cut along pencil lines with a craft knife.
5. Working on the back side of the 5-by-7 cutout, create a 1-inch mat. Measure 1-inch lines from the outer edges inward, on all four sides of the rectangle.
6. Using the metal ruler as a straight-edge, cut on the pencil lines with a craft knife.
7. Apply tacky glue to back of the corrugated mat, being sure to cover surface completely.
8. Glue corrugated mat to the front of the acrylic frame, aligning carefully.
9. Let glue dry completely.

Variation:

- Use greeting cards, wrapping paper, wallpaper, or handmade paper to decorate acrylic frames.

"Let us give thanks, by which we offer to God an acceptable worship with reverence and awe" (Heb. 12:28).

rustic picture frames

What you need:
- rustic wooden frame
- shells, twigs, stones, tree bark, cones, seeds, other found objects
- hot glue gun and glue sticks

What you do:
1. Remove glass from the frame and clean it.
2. Arrange objects on the frame to achieve the desired look.
3. Glue objects to the frame. If you're using an easel frame, be sure that the objects do not extend below the bottom of the frame, preventing it from standing correctly.
4. Let glue dry completely before inserting a picture and assembling the frame.

Variation:
- Embellish frames with buttons, silk flowers, dried flowers, marbles, crayons, toy logs, puzzle pieces, etc.

Tip:
- If children will be decorating frames, use thick-bodied tacky glue.

"'Again, truly I tell you, if two of you agree on earth about anything you ask, it will be done for you by my Father in heaven'" (Matt. 18:19).

denim heart pocket pillow

What you need:
- denim fabric
- thread (color to match fabric)
- brown paper bag or wrapping paper
- scissors
- pen
- pencil
- paint pens
- polyester fiberfill stuffing
- straight pins
- sewing machine or needle
- iron
- clean cotton cloth
- mouse pad
- acrylic paint
- ½-inch foam brush

The following instructions are for a pillow that is 12 inches-by-14 inches. You will need two paper hearts, one for the pillow and the other for the pocket

What you do:
1. Fold two pieces of paper in half and draw ½ of a heart.
2. Label one pattern piece "pillow" and the other "pocket."
3. Pin the pillow pattern to fabric and cut out two denim hearts.
4. To make the pocket pattern, cut off the top third section of the heart as indicated on the pattern.
5. Pin the pocket pattern to fabric and cut one piece.
6. To hem the top of the pocket, fold the edge over ½ inch, pin, and stitch the hem.
7. Trace small heart patterns onto white paper and cut them out.
8. Use a pen to trace the pattern onto the mouse pad.
9. Carefully cut hearts from the mouse pad, using scissors or a craft knife.
10. Brush paint onto a heart and press it firmly on the pocket.
11. Continue until all the hearts are painted.

"Wait for the Lord; be strong, and let your heart take courage; wait for the Lord" (Psalm 27:14).

12. Let paint dry completely.
13. Clean the sponge stamp and brush with water.
14. To set paint, cover the pocket with a cloth and press with an iron on cotton setting.
15. Place the pocket on top of one heart piece, right sides up, and pin them together.
16. Beginning at the top of the pocket, stitch outside edges, using a ¼-inch seam allowance.
17. Mark the center of the pocket and stitch straight down to create two pockets. Backstitch at the top of the pocket to keep the stitches from pulling loose.
18. Pin the other heart piece on top of this one; right sides together.
19. Starting on one side, stitch around the heart, using a ½-inch seam allowance. Leave a 3-inch opening to insert the stuffing.
20. Use scissors to clip around the pillow, being careful not to cut the seam.
21. Turn pillow inside out and stuff with fiberfill. Push stuffing in firmly to ensure a fluffy pillow.
22. Pin the opening together. Turn in the seams. Hand or machine stitch.
23. Place crayons, markers, pencils, books, notepads, stamps, etc., in the pockets. Personalize with paint pens.

Variation:

- If using fabric from a garment, cut around the seams and press the pieces flat with an iron.

stamp pattern

"'I am the living bread that came down from heaven. Whoever eats of this bread will live forever'" (John 6:51).

hammered flower pillow

What you need:

- cotton fabric such as cotton muslin or ticking
- thread (color to match fabric)
- polyester fiberfill stuffing
- fresh flowers and leaves
- hammer
- sewing machine or needle
- butcher or brown paper
- dull knife
- scissors
- straight pins
- fine-point permanent markers

What you do:

1. Test each leaf or petal on scrap fabric to determine the color intensity (see steps 4–7).
2. Measure and cut a 16-inch square from paper to make pillow pattern.
3. Pin pattern to the fabric and cut 2 16-inch squares.
4. Place 1 piece of fabric on a flat, hard surface (such as a cement floor). Protect other surfaces with cardboard.
5. Work with 1 or 2 leaves or petals at a time. Place a petal, facedown, on the fabric.
6. Lay a piece of white paper over the petal.
7. Tap the hammer firmly over the petal. Continue hammering until desired color intensity is reached. Lift the edge of the paper to check periodically.
8. Remove paper carefully. If the petal sticks to the fabric, use a dull knife to gently scrap it off. Let fabric dry thoroughly.
9. Use fine-point markers to add details such as stems and tendrils.
10. Pin the two fabric squares, right sides together.
11. Starting on one side, stitch around the pillow, using a ½-inch seam allowance. Leave a 3-inch opening to insert stuffing.
12. Use the scissors to clip around the pillow, being careful not to cut the seam. Cut the corners diagonally to reduce bulk.
13. Turn pillow inside out and stuff with fiberfill. Push stuffing in firmly to ensure a fluffy pillow.
14. Pin the opening together, turning seams in. Hand or machine stitch.

"Therefore be imitators of God, as beloved children, and live in love, as Christ loved us and gave himself up for us, a fragrant offering and sacrifice to God" (Eph. 5:1–2).

sweater pillow

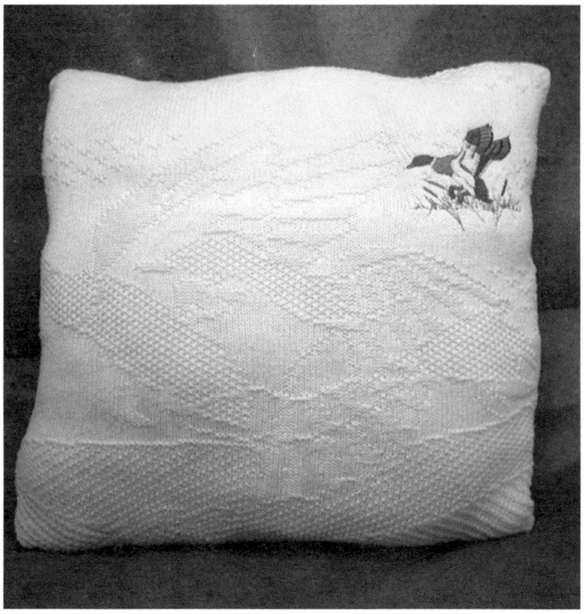

What you need:

- large or extra large sweater*
- thread (color to match sweater)
- polyester fiberfill
- brown paper bag or brown wrapping paper
- ruler
- straight pins
- scissors
- sewing machine
- needle

What you do:

1. Using the heavy brown paper, create a pattern. Measure and cut a 1-foot square from paper.
2. Lay sweater flat on a hard surface.
3. Pin the pattern in the middle of the sweater being sure fabric is flat. If the sweater is thick, you may need to cut out the pattern on the front and repeat the steps on the back.
4. Cut around the pattern.
5. Machine stitch around both pieces of the sweater, about ½-inch from the edge. This will keep edges from raveling or stretching.
6. Pin the two pieces, right sides together.
7. Beginning on one side, stitch around the pillow, leaving a 3-inch opening for stuffing.
8. Stuff pillow with fiberfill. Use small pieces, working it into the corners.
9. Pin the opening together. Turn in the seams. Hand stitch together.

Tip:

- Make a pillow using a button sweater. Sew or glue the front of the sweater together so it will not come open.

*Old cotton sweaters make soft, comfy pillows. Choose a tight-weave, machine-washable sweater.

"'Whoever wishes to be great among you must be your servant, and whoever wishes to be first among you must be your slave; just as the Son of Man came not to be served but to serve, and to give his life a ransom for many'" (Matt. 20:26–28).

friendship jar

What you need:

- jar and lid
- cellophane or tissue paper
- Life Savers® candy
- cotton ball
- rubber band
- sweet and sour candy
- candy kisses
- happy face (sticker or drawn)
- candle (birthday or votive)
- adhesive bandage strip
- eraser
- copy machine
- decorative paper
- hole punch
- cord or ribbon

What you do:

1. Arrange all items in the jars; enclosing them in cellophane or tissue paper.
2. Copy the following statements on decorative paper.
3. Punch a hole in the top left corner of the paper.
4. Thread the cord or ribbon through the hole and tie it around the jar.

Lifesaver—to remind you of the many times others need your help and you need theirs.

Cotton ball—for the rough roads ahead; seek the cushioned support of God, your family, and friends (Psalm 18:18).

Rubber band—a reminder to stay flexible.

Sweet and sour candy—to help you accept and appreciate the differences in others.

Candy kiss—to remind you that we all need hugs and kisses.

Happy face—smiling not only increases our face value, it is contagious (Proverbs 15:13).

Candle—to remind you to share your light with others (Matthew 5:14–16).

Adhesive bandage—for healing hurt feelings, yours or someone else's.

Eraser—to remind you that every day you can start over with a clean slate.

"Each one helps the other, saying to one another, 'Take courage!'" (Isa. 41:6).

fabric-covered photo album

What you need:
- 4-by-6-inch photo album
- 15-by-30-inch fabric
- 7-by-13-inch piece of fiber batting
- 28 inches of ribbon
- scissors
- straight pins
- hot glue gun and sticks

What you do:
1. In most photo albums the photo insert is attached to a piece of paper and glued to the inside spine of the album. Carefully remove the insert, leaving the paper intact. Set aside.
2. Lay the album, outside surface down, on the batting. Glue the corners of the album to the batting to hold it in place. Trim the batting to fit.
3. Lay the album, batting side down, in the center of the fabric.
4. Fold the top and bottom edges of fabric over the album and glue in place.
5. Fold the sides in toward the center of the album, tucking the edges as needed. Pin edges to secure fabric.
6. Overlap the fabric at the center of the album, trimming excess if necessary. Pin in place.
7. Glue the edges. Work in small sections, removing pins as you go. Apply glue to the inside seams of the spine and press the fabric down.
8. Glue the photo insert back onto the inside spine of the album.
9. Glue ribbon to the outside of the album.

"Welcome one another, therefore, just as Christ has welcomed you, for the glory of God" (Rom. 15:7).

scrapbook

What you need:
- 3-ring binder
- acrylic paint (base and accent colors)
- cloth ribbon
- 1-inch foam brush
- tacky glue
- rubber eraser
- craft knife
- pencil
- cardboard
- scissors
- hole punch

What you do:
1. Paint binder, inside and out. Apply several coats of paint, letting each coat dry completely.
2. Determine ribbon placement.
3. Measure the ribbon length and add ½ inch to it. Cut ribbon pieces.
4. Working from the inside of the binder, slide the end of the ribbon under the metal binder strip and glue it in place.
5. Glue ribbon around the binder and slide the other end of the ribbon under the metal strip. This will hide the cut edges of the ribbon.
6. Repeat process until all the ribbon is glued on the binder.
7. Prop the binder open and let glue dry completely.
8. With a pencil, draw stars on the eraser. Carefully cut them out with a craft knife.
9. Apply paint to the star cutout and practice stamping it on paper.
10. Determine placement of the stars and stamp the binder.
11. Paint cardboard and let dry completely.
12. Draw star shapes on the cardboard. Cut them out and glue them to the ribbon on the binder.
13. Cut a 1-inch strip of cardboard the length of the binder. Measure the distance between the rings and mark the cardboard. Punch holes in the cardboard and use this as a template for punching the holes in scrapbook paper.

Variation:
- Decorate the binder with paint pens, magazine cutouts, purchased rubber stamps, etc.

"Above all, clothe yourselves with love, which binds everything together in perfect harmony" (Col. 3:14).

bird feeder

What you need:

- 1-inch-by-6-inch-by-5-foot piece of western cedar
- electric saw
- drill
- ⅛-inch and $\frac{5}{32}$-inch drill bits
- hammer
- 36 1½-inch galvanized nails
- ruler
- red and black acrylic paint
- ½-inch foam brush
- pencil

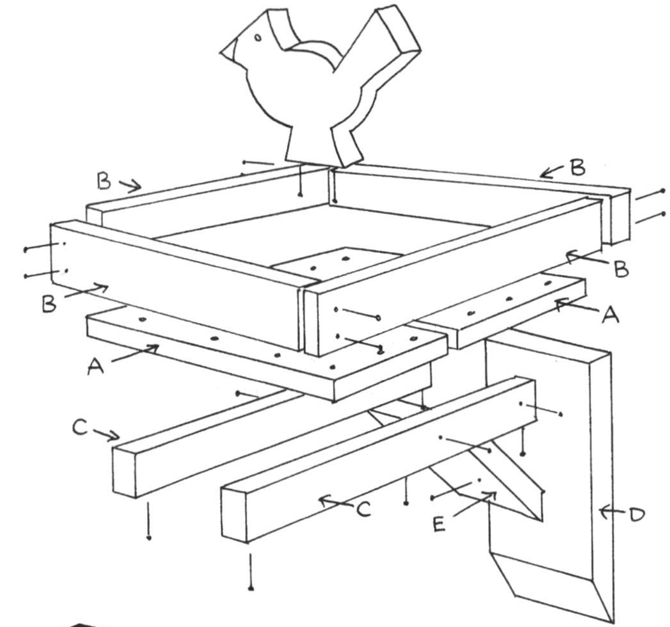

What you do:

1. Following the diagram, mark the pieces on the board.
2. Cut out the pieces with the saw.
3. Drill drainage holes in the two bottom pieces with the ⅛-inch drill bit.
4. Assemble the feeder and nail it together with the galvanized nails.
5. Trace the bird pattern (p. 65) on the board and cut it out.
6. Paint the bird and let it dry completely.
7. Nail the bird to the center of the base.

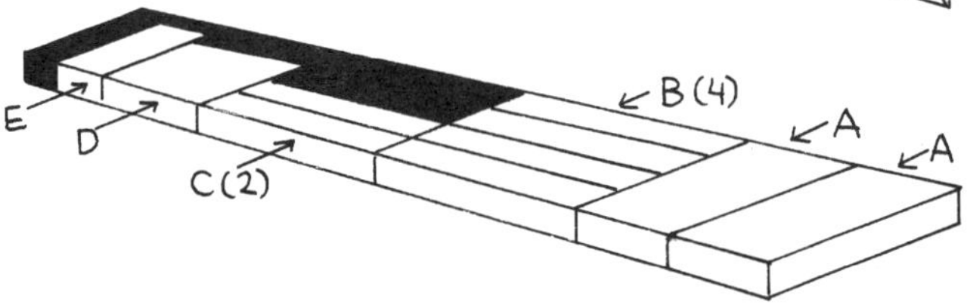

ITEM	NO. OF PIECES	SIZE	PIECE(S)
A	2	¾-by-5½-by-11 inches	Bottom
B	4	¾-by-1¼-by-11⅞ inches	Sides
C	2	¾-by-1¼-by-11⅞ inches	Bottom brace
D	1	¾-by-3½-by-7¾ inches	Mounting
E	1	¾-by-3½-by-5 inches	Brace

"'But even the hairs of your head are all counted. Do not be afraid; you are of more value than many sparrows'" (Luke 12:7).

wind chime

What you need:

- 1-by-6-by-16-inch board
- ¼-inch dowel
- 4 chimes (sold in kits)
- wood glue
- 10 1¼-inch galvanized nails
- 5 ½-inch brass nails with heads
- hammer
- electric saw
- drill and ¼-inch drill bit
- acrylic paint
- ½-inch foam brush
- nylon fishing line
- resin bird
- straw
- ¼-inch eyescrew
- pencil
- scissors

What you do:

1. Following the diagram on page 66, mark the board with the pencil.
2. Cut out the pieces with the saw.
3. Position the roof on the top of the birdhouse panel and nail it.
4. Position the base to the bottom of the birdhouse panel and nail it.
5. Paint the birdhouse and let dry.
6. Nail brass nails in the bottom of the base. *(Refer to the diagram.)* Do not hammer in completely.
7. Wrap one end of the fishing line around an outside brass nail. Thread the fishing line through one chime. Wrap the fishing line around the next nail. Continue until all the chimes are strung.
8. Adjust the chimes to the desired length and wrap the end of the fishing line around the last nail. Cut off excess line.
9. Hammer in the nails completely.
10. Following the diagram, drill the hole for the perch.
11. Cut a 1½-inch length from the dowel and glue it in the hole.
12. Glue straw under the roof and on the base of the birdhouse.
13. Glue the bird to the base.
14. Screw the eyescrew into the top.
15. Cut a 12-inch length of fishing line and thread it through the eyescrew to make a hanger.

"'The greatest among you will be your servant. All who exalt themselves will be humbled, and all who humble themselves will be exalted'" (Matt. 23:11–12).

button box sewing kit

What you need:
- cardboard jewelry box (large enough for the sewing items)
- buttons
- tacky glue
- sewing items

What you do:

1. Arrange buttons on top of box and glue in place.
2. Fill box with basic sewing items such as: black and white thread, needles, needle threader, straight pins, package of standard shirt buttons, and small scissors.

Variation:

- Ordinary boxes can be decorated to become treasures themselves. This is a great project for any age and the possibilities are limitless. Give the box to someone and teach them how to sew.

"The fear of the Lord is the beginning of knowledge; fools despise wisdom and instruction" (Prov. 1:7).

treasure box

What you need:
- natural-colored cardboard box
- jute
- shells
- hot glue gun and glue sticks

What you do:
1. Wrap jute around the box lid three times and cut it to get the correct length.
2. Hot glue jute to the box lid.
3. Arrange shells or other items from nature on top of box lid and hot glue them in place.

jewelry box

What you need:
- cardboard jewelry box
- beads
- ribbon flowers with silk leaves
- tacky glue
- scissors

What you do:
1. Apply glue in a circle on top of the box.
2. Starting in the center, wrap the beads in a circle. Cut off excess beads.
3. Glue silk flowers in the center of the circle.
4. Let glue dry completely.

"'And can any of you by worrying add a single hour to your span of life? If then you are not able to do so small a thing as that, why do you worry about the rest?'" (Luke 12:25–26).

faux ceramic vase

What you need:
- clear glass vase
- acrylic paints (2 or 3 colors)

What you do:

1. Clean vase with warm, soapy water. Dry thoroughly.
2. Squeeze small amounts of two or three colors of paint into the bottom of vase. Colors should touch. Do not put one color of paint on top of another.
3. Swirl paint around, turning the vase in different directions.
4. Cover inside of vase completely, adding more paint if necessary.
5. Let vase dry completely. (This may take several days.) Note: Do not put water in the vase because the paint is water-soluble and will peel.

Tips:

- Use acrylic paints to achieve the look of fired ceramic. Place dried or silk flowers in the vase.
- If you do not achieve the desired results, wash the vase with warm, soapy water to remove the paint.

"Blessed is anyone who endures temptation. Such a one has stood the test and will receive the crown of life that the Lord has promised to those who love him" (James 1:12).

Bath Salts, p. 6

Vinegar Soother, p. 6

Bath Crystals, p. 7

Foaming Bath Oil, p. 8

Shell Candles, p. 9

Star Candleholder, p. 10

Ribbon Candleholder, p. 11

Candle in a Cup, p. 12

Painted Candles, p. 13

Pearl Votive Candleholder, p. 14

Floral Candles, p. 15

Scripture Verse Prints, p. 16

"Families Are Like Quilts" Print, p. 17

Decoupage Frame, p. 18

Creative Acrylic Frames, p. 19

Rustic Picture Frames, p. 20

Denim Heart Pocket Pillow, p. 21

Hammered Flower Pillow, p. 23

Sweater Pillow, p. 24

Friendship Jar, p. 25

Fabric-Covered Photo Album, p. 26

Scrapbook, p. 27

Bird Feeder, p. 28

Wind Chime, p. 29

Button Box Sewing Kit, p. 30

Treasure Box, p. 31

Jewelry Box, p. 31

Faux Ceramic Vase, p. 32

Painted Bowl, p. 33

Decorative Yardstick, p. 34

Tissue Box Cover, p. 35

Apple Place Mats, p. 37

Plaid Place Mats, p. 38

Bulletin Board, p. 39

Handmade Cards, p. 40

Decoupage Popcorn Can, p. 42

Sponge-Painted Popcorn Can, p. 44

Jute-Covered Can, p. 46

Corrugated Canister, p. 47

Spice and Potpourri Topiary, p. 48

Dried Apple Roses Wreath, p. 50

Shell Wreath, p. 51

Jar Cookies, p. 52

Raffia Angels, p. 53

Flower Pin, p. 54

Snow Globes, p. 55

Gingerbread Man, p. 56

Spice Pomanders, p. 57

Magnolia Angel, p. 58

Gold Dot Ornament, p. 59

Gold Foil Star Ornament, p. 59

Lace Ornament, p. 60

Painted Ornaments, p. 60

painted bowl

What you need:
- clear glass bowl
- acrylic paints (2 or 3 colors)
- plastic food wrap
- decoupage medium
- 1-inch foam brush
- disposable foam plate

What you do:
1. Clean bowl with warm, soapy water. Dry thoroughly.
2. Squeeze small amount of 1 color of paint onto foam plate.
3. Crumple plastic wrap and dab it in paint. The plastic wrap is the paint applicator.
4. Randomly dab plastic wrap with paint inside bowl.
5. Let each coat of paint dry before applying another.
6. Repeat process with other paint colors. Use a clean piece of plastic wrap for each color.
7. Let bowl dry completely.
8. Use foam brush to apply several coats of decoupage medium to the inside of bowl to create a protective seal. Note: Do not put water in the vase because the paint is water-soluble and will peel. The bowl is not safe for food. Use for decorative purposes only.

Variations:
- Experiment with different paint combinations and applicators. Try bubble wrap, a rag, tissue paper, etc.

"For the Lord gives wisdom, from his mouth come knowledge and understanding" (Prov. 2:6).

decorative yardstick

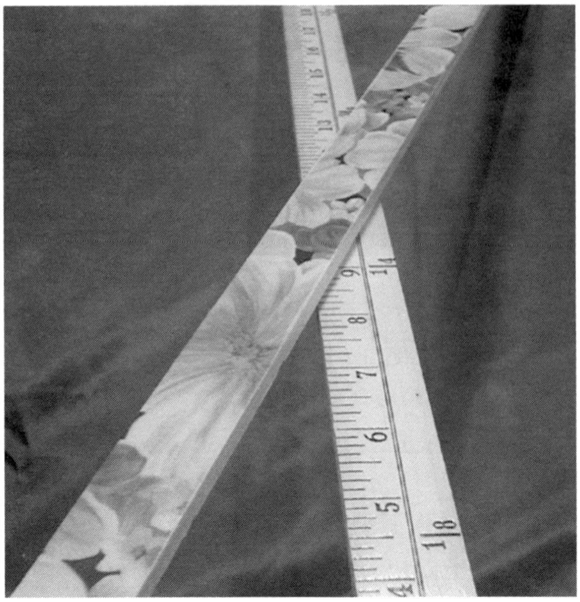

What you need:

- wooden yardstick
- ribbon (wider than yardstick)
- acrylic paint (color that matches the ribbon)
- white glue
- 1 sheet sandpaper (100 grit)
- ½-inch foam brush
- disposable foam plate
- craft knife
- masking tape

What you do:

1. If yardstick has measurements on both sides, determine which side will be used for measuring. Place a piece of masking tape on that side to avoid confusion.
2. Sand the back and edges of the yardstick so paint will stick.
3. Place a small amount of paint onto the foam plate.
4. Use the foam brush to paint the back and sides of yardstick. Be careful not to get paint on the front of the yardstick.
5. Apply several coats of paint to yardstick. Let each coat dry thoroughly.
6. Wash brush with water after each coat of paint.
7. After the last coat of paint has dried for several hours, use the foam brush to apply glue to the painted side of the yardstick.
8. Position the ribbon and press it carefully to the yardstick. Work out air bubbles. Do not glue ribbon to the sides of yardstick.
9. Let glue dry completely.
10. Working on a protected surface, trim ribbon down both edges of the yardstick using a sharp craft knife. Cut slowly and carefully.

Variation:

- Use decorative paper or fabric. Cut it wider than the yardstick, trim as instructed above and seal it with a coat of water-based varnish.

"Do not neglect to do good and to share what you have, for such sacrifices are pleasing to God" (Heb. 13:16).

tissue box cover

What you need:
- tissue box cover
- decorative tissue paper*
- 1 can spray paint (color that coordinates with the tissue paper)
- white glue
- water
- 1 sheet sandpaper (220 grit)
- 1-inch foam brush
- plastic margarine bowl and lid
- tall can or jar

What you do:
1. Paint tissue box cover following manufacturers' directions. Let it dry for 24 hours.
2. Mix 1 part white glue with 1 part water in margarine bowl. Stir until mixture is well blended. Begin with ¼ cup each and add more as needed.
3. Tear tissue paper into irregular pieces, about 3-inch-by-3-inch. Use smaller pieces for the top of the box.
4. Use foam brush to apply glue mixture to one side of box.
5. Place a piece of tissue paper on the glued area, smoothing it with the brush. The tissue paper will wrinkle, adding texture.
6. Continue placing pieces of tissue paper until all sides of the box are covered.
7. Glue tissue paper to top of box, overlapping the opening. Use your finger to press edges under for a smooth finish.
8. Smooth rough areas by brushing on more glue mixture. Smooth out wrinkles with your finger.
9. Place the box over the tall can or jar to dry. To prevent sticking, do not let box bottom rest on a surface. Let box dry completely (about 2 hours).
10. Clean brush with water and cover glue mixture for later use.
11. Apply a thin coat of glue mixture, brushing in one direction.
12. Let box dry thoroughly. Lightly sand, being careful not to cut paper.
13. Repeat the process two or three times, until surface is smooth. Do not sand final coat.

*Select paper that has a textured look, because tissue paper wrinkles.

"Bear one another's burdens, and in this way you will fulfill the law of Christ" (Gal. 6:2).

canvas place mats

What you need:

- canvas
- acrylic paints
- ruler
- scissors
- pencil
- hot glue gun and glue sticks
- 1-inch foam brush
- disposable foam plate

What you do:

1. From the finished edge of the canvas, carefully measure and draw a 14-by-20-inch rectangle.
2. To make a hem, work on back side of the canvas. Measure and draw 1-inch lines on all 4 sides of the rectangle (see diagram).
3. Cut out the 4 corners where the lines intersect.
4. Turn the edges over and glue to create a finished edge. Smooth the canvas carefully as you glue.
5. Paint the right side of the placemats with acrylic paint, covering it completely. Let dry thoroughly.

Variations:

- Let children decorate place mats by placing their hands in paint and pressing their handprints onto the canvas.
- Apply paint to one side of a leaf and stamp place mats.
- Cut shapes from sponges and use them for stamps.

"Therefore walk in the way of the good, and keep in the paths of the just" (Prov. 2:20).

apple place mats

What you need:

- canvas place mats (p. 36)
- acrylic paints (red, green, and other colors of choice)
- water-based varnish
- pencil
- ruler
- 1-inch foam brush
- disposable foam plate
- apple
- knife
- mouse pad
- scissors
- paper towels
- brown paper
- leaf pattern (at right)

What you do:

1. With pencil, lightly mark 1-inch spaces on all 4 sides of place mat. (This will be your stamping guide.)
2. Measure and cut a 1-inch square from the mouse pad.
3. Brush paint onto the square and practice stamping onto the paper.
4. Begin stamping in a corner and work around the place mat.
5. Cut an apple in half. Wipe it with paper towel to remove excess moisture.
6. Brush red paint onto the apple and practice stamping on paper.
7. Stamp the apple in each corner of the place mat, pressing firmly.
8. Trace the leaf pattern onto the mouse pad and cut it out.
9. Apply paint as before and stamp leaves near the apples.
10. Let paint dry completely.
11. Brush varnish onto the canvas to seal place mats. Apply several coats, letting each coat dry completely. Clean brush with soap and water between each coat.
12. Clean place mat with damp cloth.

"Make a joyful noise to God, all the earth; sing the glory of his name; give to him glorious praise" (Psalm 66:1–2).

plaid place mats

What you need:

- canvas place mats (p. 36)
- acrylic paints
- pear and leaf patterns (p. 66; p. 37)
- masking tape
- water-based varnish
- pencil
- ruler
- 1-inch foam brush
- disposable foam plate
- knife
- mouse pad
- scissors
- paper towels
- paper

What you do:

1. Apply strips of masking tape horizontally across the place mat, spacing evenly. Press edges of tape firmly so paint will not seep under the tape.
2. Place small amount of paint on foam plate.
3. Using the 1-inch brush, cover entire surface of the place mat with paint.
4. When paint has dried thoroughly, carefully remove masking tape.
5. Apply strips of masking tape vertically across the place mat, spacing evenly. Press edges of the tape firmly so paint will not seep under the tape.
6. Cover the entire surface of place mat with a different color paint.
7. When paint has dried thoroughly, carefully remove masking tape.
8. Trace pear and leaf patterns (p. 66; p. 37) onto paper and cut out.
9. Use a pen to trace patterns onto mouse pad and cut out with scissors or craft knife.
10. Brush paint onto pear stamp and stamp the place mat. Note: practice stamping on paper first.
11. Let paint dry completely. Clean stamp with water.
12. Brush paint onto leaf stamp and stamp leaves near the pears.
13. Let paint dry completely. Clean stamp with water.
14. Brush several coats of varnish on place mat. Allow each coat to dry completely. Clean the brush with water between each coat.

"And may the Lord make you increase and abound in love for one another and for all, just as we abound in love for you" (1 Thess. 3:12).

bulletin board

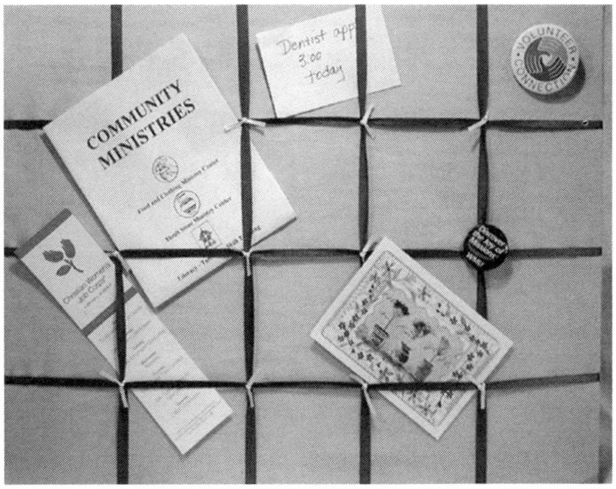

What you need:

- 16-by-20-inch artist canvas (canvas stretched over a frame)
- 20-by-24-inch fabric
- staple gun and staples
- ribbon
- tacky or fabric glue
- pencil

What you do:

1. Lay fabric right side down on a flat surface. Place canvas frame over fabric.
2. Starting on one side, pull the fabric over the frame and staple it.
3. Continue around the frame, pulling the fabric tightly, until all four sides are stapled.
4. Determine ribbon placement and lightly mark the fabric with a pencil.
5. Measure the ribbon lengths, being sure they are long enough to attach from the back of the frame.
6. Cut ribbon.
7. Staple one end of ribbon to back of frame. Stretch the ribbon across the front and staple the other end of the ribbon to the back of the frame. Staple all ribbon strips.
8. Using a different color ribbon, tie a knot at every place the ribbon intersects.
9. Glue the knot to the fabric backing and let dry thoroughly.

Variations:

- Glue buttons or beads where the ribbon intersects.
- Personalize the bulletin board by writing each family member's name on the fabric with fabric pens.

"The Lord is my strength and my shield; in him my heart trusts; so I am helped, and my heart exults, and with my song I give thanks to him" (Psalm 28:7).

handmade cards

What you need:
- paper
- scraps of fabric, corrugated paper, old greeting cards, pictures from magazines
- metal ruler
- pencil
- craft knife
- white glue or glue stick

Before you begin:
Determine the size of the card and whether the card will be folded once or twice. For example a 5-by-6-inch-high card which folds once will require a 5-by-12-inch piece of paper. The same card that folds twice will require a 10-by-12-inch piece of paper.

What you do:
1. Measure and lightly mark the paper the appropriate size.
2. Using the metal ruler as a guide, tear or cut the edges.
3. Fold the paper, creasing it carefully with your finger.
4. Decorate the card by using scrap materials.
5. Glue the design in place and let it dry thoroughly.

Card A is embellished with wallpaper and corrugated paper strips. Corrugated paper and a dried flower decorate card B. The flower hammering technique was used on textured paper and glued on the front of card C. See hammered flowers instructions (p. 23).

Tips:
- Ask paper and decorating stores to give you old paper samples.
- Experiment with different types of paper, such as wallpaper, paper bags, and wrapping paper.

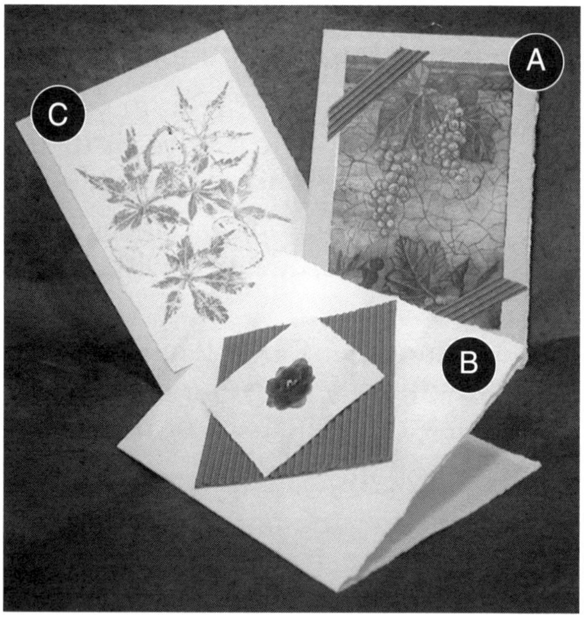

"If God is for us, who is against us? He who did not withhold his own Son, but gave him up for all of us, will he not also give us everything else?" (Rom. 8:31–32).

handmade envelope

Measure the card size (5-by-6-inches-high) and use the following formula to create a simple envelope.

What you need:

- paper
- metal ruler
- pencil
- craft knife
- white glue or glue stick

What you do:

1. Double the height and add 2 inches. For example, 6 × 2 inches = 12 inches + 2 inches = 14 inches
2. Add 1 inch to the width. For example, 5 inches + 1 inch = 6 inches
3. Mark the dimensions on the paper. Cut the edges using a ruler and craft knife.
4. Mark the card at 6 inches and 12 inches and crease.
5. Glue side edges and let dry.

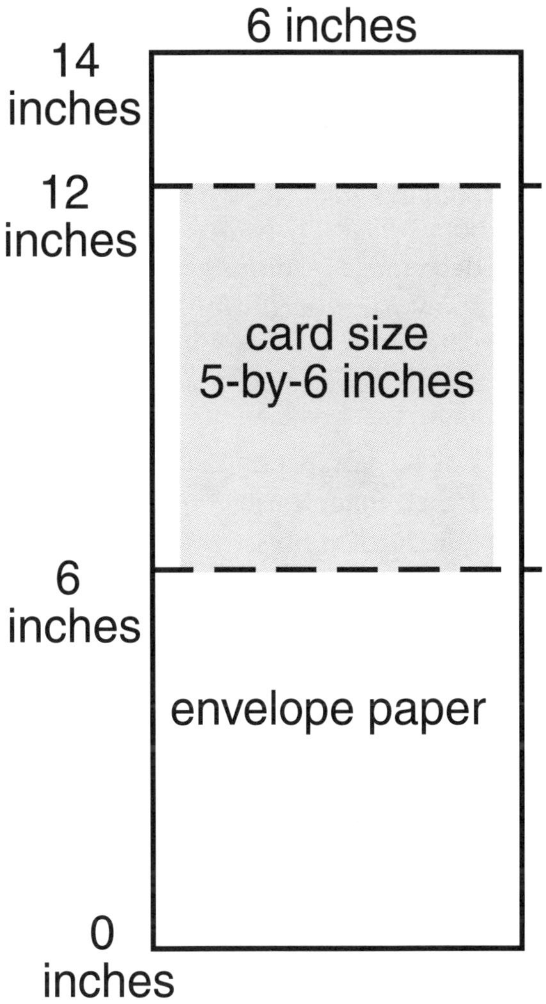

"Take my instruction instead of silver, and knowledge rather than choice gold; for wisdom is better than jewels" (Prov. 8:10–11).

decoupage popcorn can

What you need:

- popcorn can
- wrapping paper with defined images, such as flowers
- cuticle scissors or other small scissors
- decoupage medium
- spray paint (a color that coordinates with the wrapping paper)
- acrylic paint (3 colors)
- small sea sponge
- 1 sheet sandpaper (220 grit)
- 1-inch foam brush
- 3-inch foam brush
- tape
- 3 disposable foam plates
- paper towels

What you do:

1. Remove labels, clean and dry popcorn can.
2. Apply two or three coats of spray paint, following the manufacturers' directions.
3. Let the can dry for at least 24 hours to cure paint.
4. With the cuticle scissors, cut out the flowers or other images from the wrapping paper. Cut close to the image, getting as much detail as possible.
5. Wet the sea sponge and wring it out thoroughly. The sponge should be damp, not wet.
6. Squeeze a small amount of paint onto a plate.
7. Tap the sponge in paint. Remove the excess paint from the sponge by blotting it on a paper towel.
8. Tap the sponge lightly and randomly over the can, applying more paint around the top and bottom of the can, creating a background for the flowers.

"'Love the Lord your God will all your heart, and with all your soul, and with all your mind, and with all your strength'" (Mark 12:30).

9. Clean the sponge with water and blot excess water with a paper towel between each coat of paint.
10. Let that coat of paint dry, about 20 minutes.
11. Repeat steps 7 through 10, applying the other 2 colors of paint, one at a time.
12. When the sponge painting is completed, let the can dry for several hours.
13. Temporarily position the flowers by taping them to the can to create the design. Overlap the flowers and leaves to create an interesting design.
14. Use the 1-inch foam brush to apply the decoupage medium to the back of a flower.
15. Press the flower to the can with your fingers, working from the middle out, to remove any air bubbles.
16. Continue gluing flowers to the can until the design is completed.
17. Use the 3-inch foam brush to completely coat the can with decoupage medium. Sand and apply more coats, following the manufacturers' directions.
18. Let can dry for 48 hours before using.

Tip:

- To present a special gift to someone, fill the popcorn can with goodies. Include other craft items from this book.

"And God is able to make all grace abound to you, so that in all things at all times, having all that you need, you will abound in every good work" (2 Cor. 9:8 NIV).

sponge-painted popcorn can

What you need:

- popcorn can
- mouse pad
- craft knife
- scissors
- 1-inch foam brush
- 3-inch foam brush
- spray paint (base color)
- acrylic paint (red, blue, yellow)
- clear acrylic spray paint
- 1 black, medium-point, permanent marker
- ¼-inch dowel
- 1 sheet sandpaper (220 grit)
- white paper
- pencil
- 3 disposable foam plates
- paper towels

What you do:

1. Remove labels and clean popcorn can.
2. Apply two or three coats of spray paint, following the manufacturers' directions.
3. Let paint dry for 24 hours.
4. Use the 1-inch foam brush to paint a rim around the top and bottom of the can. Most cans have an indention around the can that can serve as a painting guide. Two coats of paint may be needed.
5. Clean brush with soap and water. Squeeze brush to remove as much water as possible.
6. Trace the dinosaur and star patterns (p. 45) onto white paper. Cut them out.
7. Trace the dinosaur pattern onto the mouse pad and carefully cut out the shape with scissors or a craft knife.
8. Draw a 1½-inch square on the mouse pad and cut it out.
9. With the 1-inch brush, apply blue paint to the dinosaur stamp. Practice stamping it on paper before stamping the can.

"But Jesus called the children to him and said, 'Let the little children come to me, and do not hinder them, for the kingdom of God belongs to such as these'" (Luke 18:16).

10. Stamp dinosaurs randomly around the can.
11. Clean the brush with soap and water. Squeeze the brush to remove as much water as possible.
12. Apply red paint to the star stamp. Practice stamping. Stamp stars randomly around the can.
13. Clean the brush with soap and water. Squeeze the brush to remove as much water as possible.
14. Apply yellow paint to the 1½-inch square stamp. Stamp blocks randomly around the can.
15. Clean the brush with soap and water. Squeeze the brush to remove as much water as possible.
16. Dipping the end of the dowel in the yellow paint, paint the dinosaur eyes and spots on their backs.
17. Use the black permanent marker to outline the shapes and add numbers and letters to the blocks. Let that dry completely.
18. Spray the can with the clear acrylic paint, following the manufacturers' directions.

Tips:

- Decorate popcorn tins to fit any decor.
- Use them to hold toys, diapers, etc.

"My child, do not forget my teaching, but let your heart keep my commandments" (Prov. 3:1 NIV).

jute-covered can

What you need:

- potato chip or powdered drink can with a lid
- jute
- tacky glue
- corrugated paper
- shell or smooth pebble
- pliers
- scissors
- tape measure
- ruler

What you do:

1. Use pliers to crimp down sharp edges around the inside rim of can.
2. Remove labels from the can.
3. Working from the bottom rim of the can, apply 1-inch bands of glue.
4. Wrap jute around the can, pressing down tightly as you glue and wrap to completely cover the can.
5. Do not cover the top rim with jute or the lid will not fit properly. When the can is completely covered, cut the jute with the scissors.
6. Cover the top of the lid with glue.
7. Beginning in the center of the lid, glue the jute. Wrap it around, creating a circle. Glue the jute around the rim of the lid.
8. Let the can and lid dry completely for several hours.
9. Measure around the outside of the can with the tape measure.
10. Cut a 1-inch wide strip from the corrugated paper the desired length and glue it to the can.
11. Cut two pieces of jute 2 inches longer than the corrugated strip.
12. Tie the jute strips in a bow around the corrugated strip.
13. Cut a 1½-inch square from the corrugated paper.
14. Glue the square to the center of the lid.
15. Attach a shell or pebble with glue to the center of the square to create a handle.

Tip:

- Use decorated cans to package food or other gifts. The cans become useful containers.

"See that none of you repays evil for evil, but always seek to do good to one another and to all" (1 Thess. 5:15).

corrugated canister

What you need:

- corrugated paper
- large coffee can
- hot glue gun and glue sticks
- scissors
- natural loose-weave fabric
- 3 wooden beads
- jute
- cardboard
- ruler
- tape measure
- pliers

What you do:

1. Use pliers to crimp down sharp edges around the inside rim of can.
2. Remove labels from the can.
3. Place the can on the cardboard and trace around bottom of can. Cut out the circle.
4. Trace the cardboard circle on the corrugated paper. Cut out the circle.
5. Glue the corrugated paper to the cardboard, creating the lid.
6. Measure the height and circumference of the can and mark the corrugated paper the exact measurement.
7. Using the ruler as a guide, cut the corrugated paper with a craft knife.
8. Apply hot glue to the can and attach the corrugated paper. Work in small sections.
9. Cut a 4-inch-wide strip of fabric the circumference length and glue it to the can. Be sure seams are glued well.
10. Glue a bead in the center of the back seam. Glue another bead on the front of the can, in the middle of the fabric strip.
11. Place the lid on the can. Glue one end of the jute to the center of the lid and let glue dry.
12. Wrap the jute around one of the beads on the can. Form a loop by gently pulling the jute back to the center of the lid. Glue the jute to the center of the lid.
13. Wrap the jute around the other bead. Form another loop by gently pulling the jute back to the center of the lid. Glue the jute to the center of the lid and let glue dry. Cut the jute close to glue.
14. Glue the last bead to the center of the lid to create a handle.

"Trust in the Lord with all your heart, and do not rely on your own insight" (Prov. 3:5).

spice and potpourri topiary

What you need:

- 2 3-inch foam balls
- 3-inch clay pot
- potpourri
- 8–10 6-inch cinnamon sticks
- whole cloves
- ½-inch foam brush
- tacky glue
- disposable foam plate
- sheet moss or Spanish moss
- ⅜-inch dowel
- handsaw or sharp utility knife
- 1½ yards paper ribbon
- hot glue gun and glue sticks
- 1-inch square piece of cardboard
- pencil
- scissors

What you do:

1. If necessary, clean clay pot and let it dry thoroughly.
2. Using a handsaw or utility knife, cut the dowel to measure 10 inches in length.
3. To create the topiary, insert dowel approximately 1½ inches into the 3-inch foam ball. Remove dowel. Squeeze tacky glue into hole and reinsert dowel. Set aside and let dry thoroughly.
4. Completely cover foam ball of topiary with glue. Then cover it with potpourri. Press the potpourri firmly into glue.
5. Insert whole cloves between pieces of potpourri. In other areas, sprinkle a small amount of ground ginger and allspice. Press the ground spices into glue. Set aside to dry.
6. Apply tacky glue to the inside bottom of the clay pot. Glue the cardboard to the bottom of the pot to cover the hole.
7. Apply tacky glue to the inside rim of clay pot and insert the other 3-inch foam ball, pressing firmly in place. Approximately half of the ball should be above the pot, creating a dome.

"Even before a word is on my tongue, O Lord, you know it completely" (Psalm 139:4).

8. Insert dowel into the center of the foam ball, gently pressing it through the foam until the dowel touches the bottom of the pot.
9. Make a pencil mark on the dowel at the top of the foam ball. Carefully remove the dowel.
10. Apply tacky glue to the dowel from the pencil mark to the end of the dowel.
11. Insert dowel into the hole until the dowel touches the bottom of the pot. Hold the dowel straight for a few minutes until glue sets.
12. Use the foam brush to apply a thick coat of tacky glue to the top of the foam ball in the clay pot.
13. Completely cover the foam ball with sheet moss. Let it dry completely.
14. Measure the dowel from the bottom ball to the top ball. Cut the cinnamon sticks that length.
15. Hot glue the cinnamon sticks to the dowel.
16. Tie the paper ribbon in a bow and glue it to the bottom of the potpourri ball. Trim the ends of the ribbon as desired.
17. Loosely position the ends of the bow to the moss and hot glue them in place.
18. Hot glue small pieces of cinnamon sticks around the moss and the potpourri ball, if desired.

"And whatever you do, in word or deed, do everything in the name of the Lord Jesus, giving thanks to God the Father through him" (Col. 3:17).

dried apple roses wreath

What you need:

- 2½ pounds of apples
- 6- or 8-inch grapevine wreath
- slicer or sharp knife
- 1 cup lemon juice
- 1 cup cold water
- large glass bowl
- cookie sheet
- raffia
- cinnamon sticks
- waxed paper
- oven
- paper towels
- toothpicks
- hot glue gun and glue sticks
- scissors

What you do:

1. Place cold water and lemon juice in the glass bowl.
2. Use a slicer or sharp knife to cut paper-thin slices from the apples. Cut horizontally.
3. Place the slices in the lemon water to keep them from turning brown.
4. Soak apple slices for 30 minutes.
5. Remove the slices and blot them on paper towels.
6. Line cookie sheet with waxed paper and arrange apple slices on it.
7. Bake the slices at 150°F for an hour. The slices should be leathery. If not, continue baking. Check every 15 minutes. Do not overbake or the slices will become brittle.
8. Remove the slices from the oven and let cool.
9. Fold an apple slice in half. Working from the center of the apple slice, roll it in a cone shape, creating the rose. The apple peel will be on the edge of the rose petals.
10. Insert a toothpick through the base to hold the rose in place. Let the roses dry for a few days.
11. Remove toothpicks from the roses and hot glue the roses to the wreath. Glue them in clusters, covering as much of the wreath as desired.
12. Break the cinnamon sticks into 1-inch to 2-inch pieces and glue them around the wreath.
13. Tie a raffia bow; glue it to wreath. Trim ends of raffia as desired.

"Rejoice always, pray without ceasing, give thanks in all circumstances; for this is the will of God in Christ Jesus for you" (1 Thess. 5:16–18).

shell wreath

What you need:
- grapevine wreath
- shells
- sheet moss
- florist wire or clear nylon string (fishing line)
- scissors
- hot glue gun and glue sticks
- soft cloth
- acrylic paint (optional)

What you do:
1. Wrap small pieces of moss around the wreath, securing it tightly with the florist wire or nylon string. Work in small sections, overlapping as necessary.
2. Lay the wreath down on a flat surface. Position the shells on the wreath to create a pattern.
3. Glue the shells to the wreath, overlapping them for interest.
4. Cut a 2-inch length of florist wire. Attach it to the back of the wreath, looping it to create a hanger. Twist the ends of the wire together securely.

Tip:
- Weatherworn shells can be revived with paint. Rub a small amount of acrylic paint on a shell with a damp cloth. Rub off the paint until the desired results are achieved.

"And the life I now live in the flesh I live by faith in the Son of God, who loved me and gave himself for me" (Gal. 2:20).

jar cookies

What you need:

- quart jar with lid
- ⅔ teaspoon salt
- 1⅛ cups flour
- ⅓ cup cocoa
- ⅔ cup brown sugar
- ⅔ cup sugar
- ½ cup semisweet chocolate chips
- ½ cup walnuts
- trim—optional (fabric, raffia, ribbon)

What you do:

1. Wash the quart jar and the lid in warm, soapy water and dry thoroughly.
2. Layer the ingredients in the following order.

   ⅔ teaspoon salt
   ½ + ⅛ cups flour
   ⅓ cup cocoa
   ½ cup flour
   ⅔ cup brown sugar
   ⅔ cup sugar
   ½ cup semisweet chocolate chips
   ½ cup walnuts
3. Seal jar with lid.
4. Decorate jar with trim, if desired.
5. Attach a tag to the jar with instructions.

Instruction tag

Combine the contents of jar with:
1 teaspoon vanilla
⅔ cup vegetable oil
3 eggs

Pour batter into a greased pan and bake at 350°F. Bake 32–37 minutes for 7-by-11-inch pan or 27–32 minutes for a 9-inch pan. Bon appétit!

"'If you, then, though you are evil, know how to give good gifts to your children, how much more will your Father in heaven give good gifts to those who ask him!'" (Matt. 7:11 NIV).

raffia angels

What you need:
- bundle of raffia
- 1-inch foam ball
- fabric
- glue
- scissors

What you do:

1. Cut about 33 pieces of raffia 18 inches long. Three pieces will be used to tie around the body.
2. Tie a 30-piece bundle of raffia in the middle with another piece of raffia and fold it at at the tie. The ends of the tie will become part of the body.
3. Insert the foam ball just below the knot. Using another piece of raffia, secure the foam ball. This becomes the head and neck. Wrap the bundle of raffia around the foam ball and spread it evenly. The ends of the tie will become part of the body.
4. Cut about 15 pieces of raffia 11 inches long to make arms.
5. Divide the body in half and slide the arms in, centering them between the front and back under the neck.
6. Tie the body under the arms with a piece of raffia.
7. Tie the arms, about 3 inches from the end. Trim the raffia to create hands.
8. Cut a 5-by-11-inch piece of fabric and fray the edges.
9. Fold the fabric in half lengthwise. Cut a small hole in the center of the fold for the head opening.
10. Place the fabric over the head. Gather it under the arms and tie it with another piece of raffia, forming a waist.
11. Trim the bottom of the body to about 1 inch below the dress.
12. Cut about 15 pieces of raffia 20 inches long for the wings.
13. Tie the raffia in a bow and glue it to the back of the body.
14. To create the halo, twist three pieces of raffia in a circle.
15. Overlap the ends and glue together.
16. Glue halo to the back of the head.
17. Glue hands together at the wrists.

"'For where two or three are gathered in my name, I am there among them'" (Matt. 18:20).

flower pin

What you need:

- small silk or ribbon flowers
- 6–8 small silk leaves
- small teardrop pearls
- pin back (sold in jewelry department at craft stores)
- felt
- tacky glue
- thin cardboard (1½-by-2½ inches)

What you do:

1. Trace oval pattern on a piece of cardboard and felt. Cut both the cardboard and felt pattern.
2. Glue silk leaves around the outside of the cardboard, overlapping if necessary. Allow about ¼ inch of the leaf to extend beyond the cardboard, creating a background for the flowers.
3. Arrange flowers and glue them onto the cardboard.
4. Glue pearls between the flowers, as desired.
5. Glue felt onto the back of the pin.
6. Position the pin back and glue to the felt.
7. Let pin dry completely.

pattern for pin back

"Therefore encourage one another and build up each other, as indeed you are doing" (1 Thess. 5:11).

snow globes

What you need:

- empty condiment jar with lid
- figurine
- distilled water
- glycerin
- white crystal glitter (looks like snow)
- spray paint
- multipurpose cement glue
- sandpaper
- paper towels

What you do:

1. Remove label, and wash condiment jar and lid with warm, soapy water.
2. Paint the outside of the lid, if desired.
3. Let paint dry thoroughly.
4. Sand the inside of the lid, just enough to make the surface rough.
5. Glue the figurine to the inside of the lid.
6. Let glue dry completely.
7. Fill jar almost to top with distilled water. Add ½ teaspoon of glitter.
8. Add a few drops of glycerin to water, screw on the lid, and shake. Glycerin keeps the glitter from falling too quickly. Too much glycerin will cause the glitter to stick to the bottom of the jar.
9. Add a few drops of glycerin at a time, screw the lid on the jar, and shake it. When the solution is correct the glitter will swirl around like snow.
10. Remove the lid and dry it thoroughly.
11. Apply glue to the inside rim of the lid and screw it on tightly.
12. Leave the jar upright, lid on top, until the glue has dried completely (about 12 hours).

Tips:

- Use small condiment jars to create snow globes. Large jars can be too heavy.
- Be sure the figurine will fit in the lid with enough room for the jar to fit around it.

"'It is written, "One does not live by bread alone, but by every word that comes from the mouth of God"'" (Matt. 4:4).

gingerbread man

What you need:

- poster board
- thin craft wood
- band saw
- drill and ¼-inch drill bit
- pattern (p. 65)
- ribbon or cord
- acrylic paint—white, black, green, red, and light brown
- fine sandpaper (220 grit)
- ½-inch foam brush
- small craft brush
- disposable foam plate
- ¼-inch dowel
- ⅛-inch dowel
- 1/16-inch dowel
- paint pen or permanent marker

What you do:

1. Trace the pattern onto poster board and cut it out.
2. Trace the poster board pattern onto the wood and use a band saw to cut out the gingerbread man.
3. Drill the hole for the ribbon.
4. Sand the gingerbread man all over, especially the edges.
5. Mix brown paint and a little water on the foam plate to create a stain.
6. Using the foam brush, apply stain, completely covering the figure.
7. Let stain dry completely.
8. Following the pattern, paint the vest and icing.
9. Dip the ¼-inch dowel in white paint and dot eyes on the face. Let dry thoroughly.
10. Dip the ⅛-inch dowel in black paint and dot the center of each eye. Let dry thoroughly.
11. Dip the 1/16-inch dowel in red paint and dot the nose and corners of the mouth.
12. Using a small craft brush, paint the smile with black paint.
13. Clean brush with water.
14. Paint white dots in the eyes and nose for highlights. Let dry thoroughly.
15. Cut an 8-inch length of ribbon, thread through the hole and tie.
16. Using a paint pen or permanent marker, write a name across the vest to personalize it.

"When I was a child, I thought like a child, I reasoned like a child; when I became an adult, I put an end to childish ways" (1 Cor. 13:11).

spice pomanders

What you need:

- 6–8 ounces cinnamon
- 1 cup applesauce, room temperature
- cookie cutters (outline shapes are best)
- cookie sheet
- oven
- waxed paper or aluminum foil
- large bowl
- drinking straw
- rolling pin
- ¼-inch wide ribbon

What you do:

1. Measure 2 to 3 tablespoons of cinnamon and set aside.
2. Pour the remainder of the cinnamon into a bowl.
3. Add ½ cup of applesauce and begin mixing with your hands. The mixture will be dry and crumbly.
4. Continue to add applesauce, mixing well each time until the mixture begins to stick together.
5. Pinch off about ¼ of the mixture and place the rest in a resealable plastic bag.
6. Sprinkle a little cinnamon on the work surface. Knead the mixture until it becomes pliable.
7. Roll dough to ¼-inch thickness. (If there are cracks in the dough, knead it some more and roll again.)
8. Cut out the dough with cookie cutters.
9. Use the straw to cut a hole in the dough for the ribbon, being careful not to get too close to the edge.
10. Cover the cookie sheet with waxed paper or aluminum foil.
11. Gently lift the cutout, pat the edges smooth with your fingers, and place it on the cookie sheet. Continue until all dough shapes are cut.
12. Place cookie sheet in oven and bake for about 1 hour at 150°F.
13. After the first hour, turn the cutouts over and bake for another hour. Then turn off the oven and leave the cookie sheet in the oven overnight.
14. Cut ribbon in 10-inch lengths.
15. Thread ribbon through the holes in the shapes and tie knots.

Tips:

- Use these to decorate packages or add to baskets and wreaths.
- Also use as Christmas ornaments.
- Store in an airtight plastic bag.

"And he said to them, 'Go into all the world and proclaim the good news to the whole creation'" (Mark 16:15).

magnolia angel

What you need:

- 6- to 8-inch artificial magnolia blossom with bendable petals and leaves, and a center pod
- 24-inch-long piece of tulle*
- Spanish moss
- 3-inch length of gold star garland or gold wire
- 1 yard of gold cord
- 1-by-2-inch piece of lightweight cardboard
- gold paint
- ½-inch foam brush
- tacky glue
- scissors
- wire cutters

What you do:

1. Flatten the flower leaves and petals.
2. Hold the stem and bend the pod upward to create the head.
3. Cut a 6-inch piece of gold cord; tie the ends together. Glue center of the loop to the top of the head.
4. Glue Spanish moss to the head to create hair.
5. Bend the garland in a quarter-sized circle to make the halo. Glue it to the top of the head.
6. Select two small center flower petals. Fold each in half lengthwise with edges up. Bend the petals around and glue together to form arms.
7. Pull an outside flower petal up behind the head.
8. Pull one outside petal to the right and another to the left of the pod, creating wings.
9. Pull all other petals to the bottom, creating a skirt.
10. Use wire cutters to remove all but the two largest leaves.
11. Bend ⅓ of the leaf tip back on both leaves. Pull the leaves up slightly above the wings.
12. Fold tulle in half. Tie in a large bow and glue it to the back of the angel.
13. Paint one side of the cardboard and let it dry. Repeat for other side.
14. Fold cardboard in half to make the songbook.
15. Place it inside the arms and glue.
16. Tie a bow with the remaining piece of gold cord and glue it under the arms.

*Sold in bridal department of fabric store.

"Do not neglect to show hospitality to strangers, for by doing that some have entertained angels without knowing it" (Heb. 13:2).

gold dot ornament

What you need:

- clear glass ornament balls*
- gold glitter glue
- straws
- block of foam

What you do:

1. Remove cap from ornament and apply glitter glue randomly in small dots to the clean glass ball.
2. Insert a straw in the foam block and place the glass ball over the straw to dry.
3. When completely dry, reattach the cap.

*See instructions on page 67 for recycling old glass ornaments.

gold foil star ornament

What you need:

- clear glass ornament balls*
- self-adhesive gold foil stars
- 12-inch square piece of tulle**
- small rubber band
- gold cord

What you do:

1. Remove cap from ornament and place stars randomly around the clear glass ball.
2. Gather tulle around the ball. Secure at the top with rubber band.
3. Tie gold cord around the ball. Remove the rubber band if desired.
4. Reattach the cap.

*See instructions on page 67 for recycling old glass ornaments.
**Sold in bridal department of fabric store.

"And now faith, hope, and love abide, these three; and the greatest of these is love" (1 Cor. 13:13).

lace ornament

What you need:
- clear glass ornament ball*
- bridal lace with floral pattern
- sewing scissors
- white glue
- small pearls

What you do:
1. Remove cap from ornament.
2. Cut out the flower shapes from the lace using sharp scissors.
3. Apply glue to the back of the cut-out and press firmly onto the glass ball. Let dry completely.
4. Dot glue on the lace and add pearls.
5. Reattach the cap.

*See instructions on page 67 for recycling old glass ornaments.

painted ornaments

What you need:
- clear glass ornament ball*
- acrylic paints (two or three colors)
- egg carton

What you do:
1. Turn the egg carton upside down and cut holes in each cup. You will use the egg carton to hold the ornaments as they dry.
2. Remove the cap from ornament and squeeze small amounts of 2 or 3 colors of paint into the bottom of the glass ornament. The colors should touch, but don't put one color on top of the other.
3. Swirl paint around by turning the ball in different directions. Cover the inside completely, adding additional paint if necessary.
4. Turn the glass ornament ball upside down in a hole in the egg carton. Work on a protected surface because excess paint will drain from the ornament ball.
5. Let the ornament ball dry completely. This may take several days. Reattach the cap.

Variations:
- Create unique and colorful ornaments by experimenting with various color combinations. Metallic paints create unusual effects.

"'Don't store up for yourselves treasures on earth, where moth and rust consume, and where thieves break in and steal'" (Matt. 6:19).

peppermint bark

What you need:

- 2 pounds white melting chocolate
- 24–36 peppermint discs or 12 candy canes
- ¼ teaspoon peppermint flavoring
- plastic sealable bag
- heatproof bowl
- saucepan
- large spoon
- 11-by-17-inch baking pan
- waxed paper
- stovetop

What you do:

1. Place the peppermint candy in a plastic bag; remove the air and seal.
2. Beat the candy with a large spoon until it is crushed into small pieces.
3. Cover baking pan with waxed paper and set aside.
4. Add about 3 inches of water to the saucepan and place the heatproof bowl in this pan.
5. Cut the chocolate into small pieces and place them in the bowl.
6. Bring water to a full boil and cook until the chocolate melts. Add water to the bottom pan as needed.
7. Stir chopped candy into the melted chocolate.
8. Add peppermint flavoring and stir well.
9. Remove the pan from the heat and pour the mixture onto the baking pan.
10. Chill until firm and break into small pieces.

"So that by God's will I may come to you with joy and be refreshed in your company. The God of peace be with all of you. Amen" (Rom. 15:32–33).

Scripture verse print

See instructions on page 16.

"I lift up my eyes to the hills—where
does my help come from?
My help comes from the Lord, the
Maker of heaven and earth"
(Psalm 121: 1–2 NIV).

Scripture verse print

See instructions on page 16.

"The Lord gives perfect peace
to those whose faith is firm"
(Isa. 26:3 CEV).

"families are like quilts" print

See instructions on page 17.

Families are like quilts—
Lives pieced and stitched together,
Colored with happiness and
tears
Bound by memories
and love.

Bird for bird feeder
See instructions on page 28.

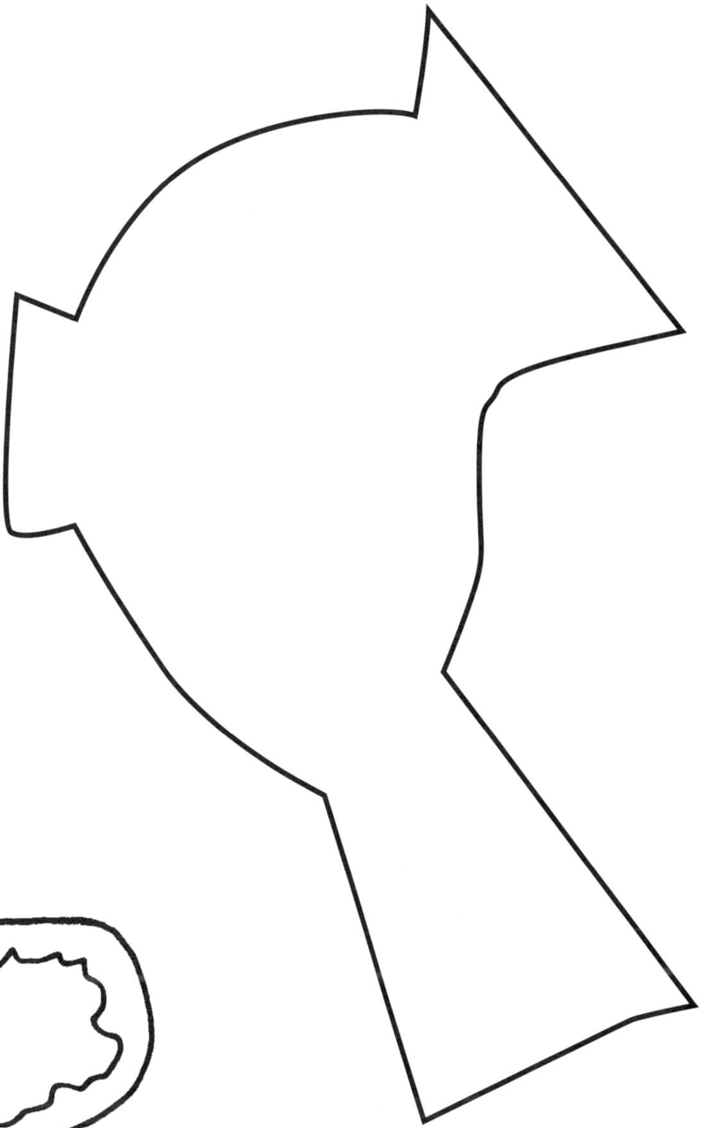

Gingerbread man
See instructions on page 56.

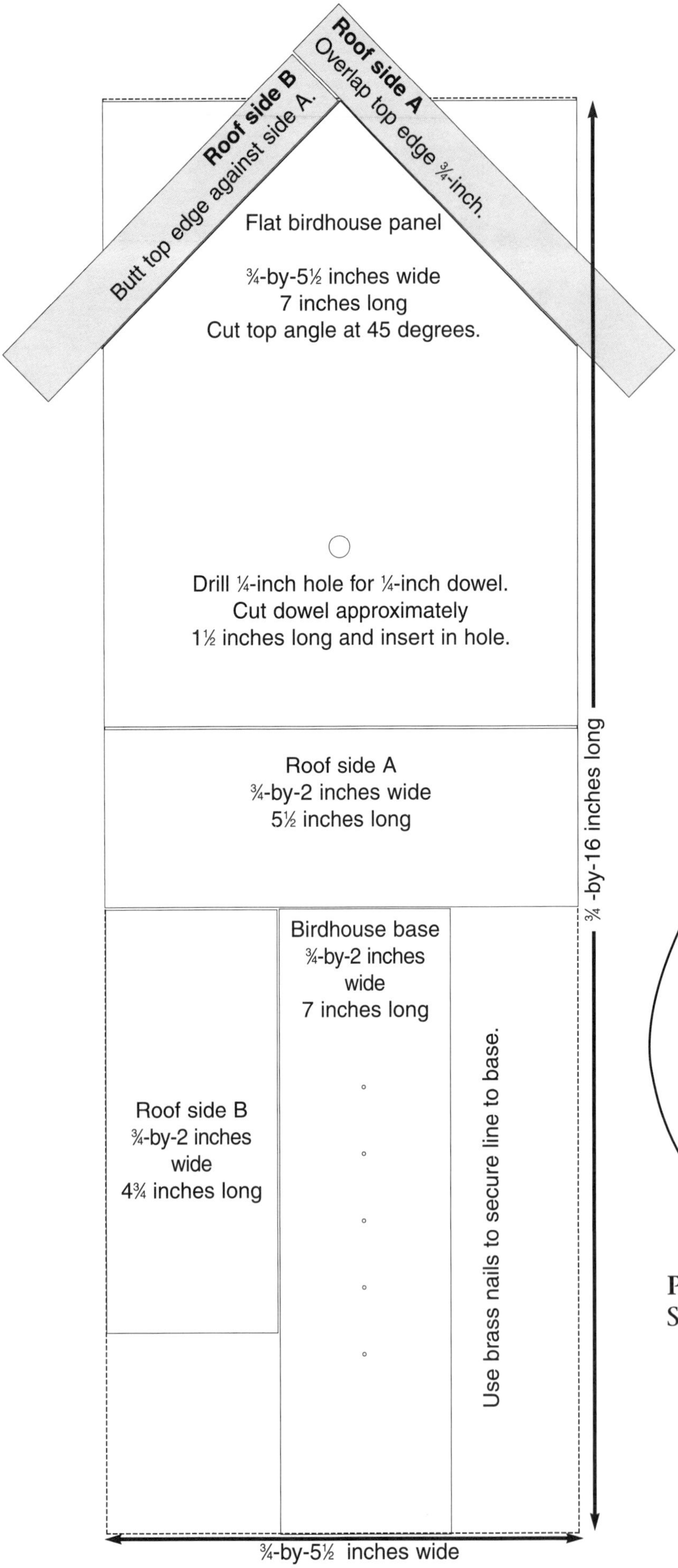

Pattern for wind chime
See instructions on page 29.

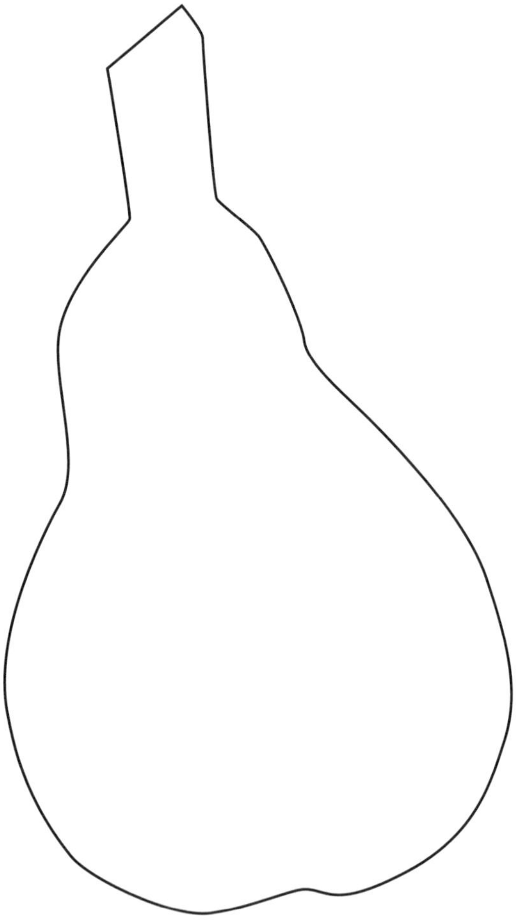

Pear pattern
See instructions on page 38.

instructions for recycling old glass ornaments

What you need:

- kitchen sink or large pan or bowl
- dishwashing liquid soap
- chlorine bleach
- water
- rubber gloves
- sand or other abrasive material
- spray paint

What you do:

1. Remove caps from the ornaments.
2. Spray paint caps, if desired, following manufacturer's directions.
3. Immerse ornaments in hot, soapy water to remove the outer paint. There will still be paint on the inside of the ornament. Rinse well and set aside.
4. Mix one part chlorine bleach to four parts hot water. Fill ornaments with the bleach and water solution. Protect hands by wearing rubber gloves.
5. Let ornaments soak in solution for several hours.
6. The edges of the ornaments are sharp. Wear gloves for protection. Working with one ornament at a time, pour about ½ of the solution out of the ornament. Pour some sand inside the ornament, hold your thumb over the opening, swish the water and sand around until paint is removed.
7. Wash the ornament. Turn the ornament upside down on a towel and let dry completely.

Tip:

- Old Christmas ornaments can be recycled by removing the paint from the glass and painting the caps if necessary.

"Love is patient; love is kind; love is not envious or boastful or arrogant" (1 Cor. 13:4).